LIGHT

LIGHT

EDITED BY MICHAEL ANDERSON

Britannica
Educational Publishing

IN ASSOCIATION WITH

ROSEN
EDUCATIONAL SERVICES

Published in 2013 by Britannica Educational Publishing
(a trademark of Encyclopædia Britannica, Inc.)
in association with Rosen Educational Services, LLC
29 East 21st Street, New York, NY 10010.

Distributed exclusively by Rosen Educational Services.
For a listing of additional Britannica Educational Publishing titles, call toll free (800) 237-9932.

First Edition

Britannica Educational Publishing
J.E. Luebering: Director, Core Reference Group, Encyclopædia Britannica
Adam Augustyn: Assistant Manager, Encyclopædia Britannica

Anthony L. Green: Editor, Compton's by Britannica
Michael Anderson: Senior Editor, Compton's by Britannica
Andrea R. Field: Senior Editor, Compton's by Britannica
Sherman Hollar: Senior Editor, Compton's by Britannica

Marilyn L. Barton: Senior Coordinator, Production Control
Steven Bosco: Director, Editorial Technologies
Lisa S. Braucher: Senior Producer and Data Editor
Yvette Charboneau: Senior Copy Editor
Kathy Nakamura: Manager, Media Acquisition

Rosen Educational Services
Nicholas Croce: Editor
Nelson Sá: Art Director
Cindy Reiman: Photography Manager
Karen Huang: Photo Researcher
Brian Garvey: Designer, Cover Design
Introduction by Nicholas Croce

Library of Congress Cataloging-in-Publication Data

Light/edited by Michael Anderson. — 1st ed.
    p. cm. — (Introduction to physics)
"In association with Britannica Educational Publishing, Rosen Educational Services."
Includes bibliographical references and index.
ISBN 978-1-61530-840-8 (library binding)
1. Light—Juvenile literature. I. Anderson, Michael, 1972–
QC360.L53 2013
535 — dc23

                                                                                        2012010241

CONTENTS

It's hard to imagine a world without light. Most of us, however, take for granted just how complex and intriguing this form of energy is. This volume investigates the nature of light, from its basic behaviors such as reflection and refraction to its relationship to the concepts of space and time.

The properties of light have puzzled scientists for centuries. Isaac Newton believed that light was composed of particles. Christiaan Huygens believed it traveled in the form of a wave. Even up to the early 20th century, scientists could not explain why light conformed to both particle and wave theory. It was not until 1924 that Louis de Broglie put forth the idea that both theories were necessary to explain the properties of light.

Light is one of several forms of energy that together are known as electromagnetic (EM) radiation. The various forms of EM radiation are arranged on a spectrum according to their wavelengths, which fall within a very wide range. Light is the form of EM radiation that is visible to the human eye. It occupies a very narrow band within the broad EM spectrum, from about 700 nanometers (nm; billionths of a meter) down to about 400 nm. The other forms of EM radiation, which are invisible to the human eye, include gamma rays, X-rays, ultraviolet radiation, infrared radiation, and radio waves. In other words, the light we see when watching a sunset or reading a book is only a portion of the radiation that exists around us.

Without light, vision would be impossible. We see the objects around us, such as our friends' faces or a dog running down the street, only when light rays bounce off those objects' surfaces and travel to our eyes. The colors of those objects are a result of the wavelengths of the light waves that reach our eyes. Light of different wavelengths appears as different colors. For example, red light has a long wavelength, and violet light has a short wavelength. Normally all the wavelengths, or colors, travel together as white light, but white light separates into its individual colors when it strikes objects. When white light strikes a ripe tomato, for instance, mostly red wavelengths reflect off the tomato, while the other colors are absorbed. This causes the tomato to look red.

Another aspect of light that has proved central to the study of physics is its speed. Measuring the speed of light was a long-standing challenge for scientists. In 1905 Albert Einstein made a breakthrough. As part of his theory of special relativity, he put forth that the speed of light is the same for all observers. Since then, the speed of light has been considered a fundamental constant of nature. In Einstein's famous relativity equation, $E=mc^2$, the speed of light (c) serves as a constant linking the formerly separate concepts of mass (m) and energy (E). The work of later scientists refined measurements of the speed of light, which was eventually defined at exactly 299,792,458 meters (186,282 miles) per second.

This volume explores the mysterious properties of light, from its physical characteristics to its intriguing behavior. It provides a strong foundation for the study of this crucial and complex form of energy, which fundamentally shapes our everyday lives and, on the grandest scale, provides a window on the structure of the universe.

CHAPTER 1

THE FUNDAMENTALS OF LIGHT

One of the most familiar and important forms of energy is light. Nothing is visible to humans when light is totally absent. But light is even more important for other reasons. Many scientists believe that millions of years ago light from the Sun triggered the chemical reactions that led to the development of life on Earth. Without light the living things now on Earth would be unable to survive. Light from the Sun provides energy for life on Earth. Plants change the energy of sunlight into food energy. When light rays strike a green plant, some of their energy is changed to chemical energy, which the plant uses to make food out of air and minerals. This process is called photosynthesis. Very nearly all living organisms on Earth depend directly or indirectly on photosynthesis for their food energy.

Some of the energy of sunlight is absorbed by Earth's atmosphere or by Earth itself.

Much of this energy is then changed to heat energy, which helps warm the planet, keeping it in the temperature range that living things have adapted to.

LIGHT AND ELECTROMAGNETIC RADIATION

Different kinds of light are visible to different species. Humans see light in what is called the visible range. It includes all the colors beginning with red and continuing through orange, yellow, green, blue, and violet. Some people can see farther into the violet region or the red region than other people. Some animals have a different sensory range. Pit vipers, for example, have sense organs (pits) that "see" rays that humans feel as heat. These rays are called infrared radiation. Bees, on the other hand, not only see some of the colors that humans see but are also sensitive to ultraviolet radiation, which is beyond the range visible to humans. So, though human eyes cannot detect them, infrared rays and ultraviolet rays are related to visible light. Instruments have been built that can detect and photograph objects by means of infrared rays or ultraviolet rays. X-rays, which can also be used to photograph objects, are also related to light.

The atmosphere causes light to be displayed in breathtaking ways, such as during a sunset. iStockphoto/Thinkstock

Scientists have learned that all these forms of energy and many other kinds of energy, such as radio waves, microwaves, and gamma rays, have the same structure. They all consist of electrical and magnetic fields that work together in a special way to form electromagnetic radiation.

SOURCES OF LIGHT

Unlike many other animals, humans depend primarily on sight to learn about the world around them. During the day early peoples could see by the light that came from the Sun, but night brought darkness and danger. One of the most important steps people have taken to control their

A rainbow forms when the Sun's rays strike raindrops falling from distant rain clouds. A ray of white sunlight is actually composed of all the colors of the spectrum. Inside the raindrops, the ray is separated into the individual colors that make it up: violet, blue, green, yellow, orange, and red. **Jan Mika/Shutterstock.com**

environment occurred when they learned to conquer the dark by controlling fire—a source of light.

Torches, candles, and oil lamps are all sources of light. They depend on a chemical reaction—burning—to release the energy we see as light. Plants and animals that glow in the dark—glowworms, fireflies, and some mushrooms—change the chemical

THE ELECTROMAGNETIC SPECTRUM

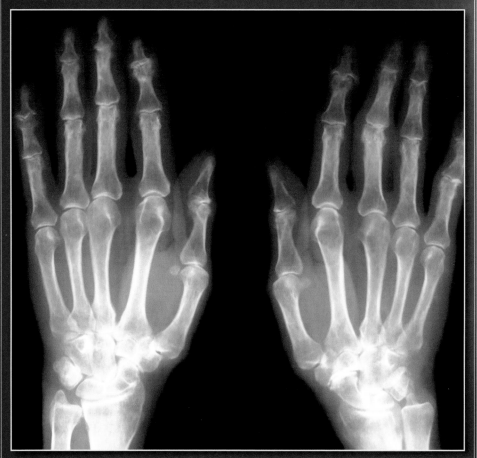

An X-ray revealing the bones of human hands. xpixel/Shutterstock.com

Electromagnetic (EM) radiation is one of three general categories of radiation (the others being mechanical radiation and particle radiation). EM radiation is sometimes referred to as light or radiant energy. It can travel through a vacuum as easily as it can through air and often passes through materials, such as glass, that are thought of as solid.

Sunlight is a familiar example of EM radiation. Its energy is used in many ways by almost all life on Earth. Sight is made possible by the reflection of visible light from objects to the eye. The Sun's heat, which is infrared radiation, bathes Earth and creates climates that can sustain life in many regions. Ultraviolet (UV) light interacts with cells of the skin to stimulate the production of vitamin D.

The orderly arrangement of EM radiation according to the amount of energy being moved is called the electromagnetic spectrum. Starting with lowest energy (longest wavelength) and moving up to highest energy (shortest wavelength), the subcategories of the electromagnetic spectrum are radio waves, infrared radiation, visible light, ultraviolet radiation, X-rays, and gamma rays.

energy stored in their tissues to light energy. Such creatures are called bioluminescent. Electric lightbulbs and neon lights change electrical energy, which may be produced by chemical, mechanical, or atomic energy, into light energy.

Light sources are necessary for vision. An object can be seen only if light travels from the object to an eye that can sense it. When the object is itself a light source, it is called luminous. Electric lights are luminous. The Sun is a luminous object because it is a source of light. An object that is not itself a source of light must be illuminated by

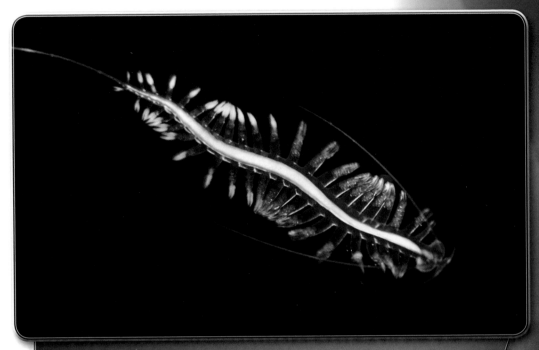

The bioluminescent sea worm Tomopteris pacifica. David Fleetham/Visuals Unlimited/Getty Images

a luminous object before it can be seen. The Moon is illuminated by the Sun. It is visible only where the Sun's rays hit it and bounce off toward Earth—or to an observer in a spacecraft.

In a completely dark room, nothing is visible. When a flashlight is turned on, its bulb and objects in its beam become visible. If a bright overhead bulb is switched on, its light can bounce off the walls, ceiling, floor, and furniture, making them and other objects in its path visible. Heating some things causes them to give off visible light rays as well as invisible heat rays. This is the case for electric-light filaments, red-hot burners on electric stoves, and glowing coals. The light of such objects is incandescent. Other light sources emit light energy but no heat energy. They are known as luminescent, or cold light, sources. Neon and fluorescent lights are luminescent.

MEASURING LIGHT

The total amount of light given off by a light source is called the luminous flux. It is measured in units called lumens. For example, a 100-watt incandescent lightbulb or a 26-watt compact fluorescent bulb emits about 1,600 lumens.

People are often more interested in measuring the amount of light that falls on a surface—for example, a desktop or the floor and walls of a room—than in measuring the total amount of light that leaves a light fixture. This measure is called illumination. When distance is measured in feet, the illumination of a surface is expressed in foot-candles. A foot-candle equals one lumen per

A powerful theater spotlight. Matusciac Alexandru/ Shutterstock.com

square foot. The international counterpart of the foot-candle is the lux, a metric unit that measures illumination in meters instead of feet. A lux equals one lumen per square meter. One foot-candle equals 10.76 lux.

The clarity with which an object can be seen depends in part on how well it is illuminated. The intensity of the light—that is, the amount of light given off by the light source

The area illuminated by a lamp illustrates how light spreads over distance. Andy Dean Photography/Shutterstock.com

in the direction of the object—is one factor in determining how well the object will be illuminated. Intensity is measured in units called candelas. A candela (once called a candle) used to be defined as the amount of light given off by a carefully constructed wax candle. It is now more precisely defined as one lumen per steradian. (A steradian is the portion of the surface of a sphere that is equal to the square of the sphere's radius divided by the total surface area.)

Other factors that affect how well an object will be illuminated are the slant of the illuminated surface in relation to the light source and the distance between the surface and the source. As a light beam travels outward from most light sources—the exceptions include lasers and searchlights—the beam spreads to cover a larger area. Distance greatly weakens illumination from such sources. The same amount of light will cover a larger area if the surface it reaches is moved farther away. This results in weaker illumination, following the inverse-square law. If the distance from the source is doubled, the amount of light falling on a given area is reduced to one-fourth—the inverse of two squared. If the distance is tripled, the area receives only one-ninth of the original illumination—the inverse of three squared.

CHAPTER 2

LIGHT AND MATTER

The way substances look depends greatly on what happens when light hits them. It is possible to see through transparent substances more or less clearly because light can pass through them without being scattered or stopped. Light that bounces off the objects behind a transparent substance can pass right through it almost as if it were not in the way. Clear window glass and clean water are transparent.

With opaque substances, only the surfaces are visible. Light cannot pass through them, and it is not possible to see through them. Opaque substances either absorb or reflect light. The light energy they absorb usually turns into heat and raises their temperature. Mercury, steel, and wood are examples of opaque substances. Translucent substances permit some light to pass through them, but the light is scattered, and the images of objects behind them are not retained. Usually, if translucent substances

Sunlight penetrating the ocean's surface. Stephan Kerkhofs/
Shutterstock.com

are made thinner, they become transparent; if they are made thicker, they become opaque. Frosted lightbulbs, waxed paper, and some kinds of curtain materials are translucent.

REFLECTION

Reflection occurs when a light ray hits a surface and bounces off. The angle at which the ray hits the surface is equal to the angle at which it bounces off. If the surface is made very flat and smooth by polishing, all the light rays bounce off in the same direction. This type of reflection is called regular, specular, or mirror reflection. A mirror surface forms an image of things that reflect light onto it. This occurs because the light rays maintain the same pattern, except reversed from left to right, that they possessed before being reflected.

A boy viewing his reflection in a mirror. Carlos Davila/ Photographer's Choice/ Getty Images

Sunlight reflecting off the ocean's surface. Vibrant Image Studio/ Shutterstock.com

Mirrors are usually made of smooth glass with a thin layer of a shiny metal such as silver bonded to the rear side.

When an opaque surface is rough, even on the microscopic level, the light rays that hit it are scattered, causing the surface itself to become visible. This is diffuse, or irregular, reflection. If a piece of raw steel with a rough opaque surface is polished smooth and flat, it reflects light rays regularly and takes on the qualities of a mirror.

REFRACTION AND DISPERSION

Light travels in a straight line as it passes through a transparent substance. But when it moves from one transparent material to another of different density—for example,

MIRRORS

Any glass or other smooth, polished surface that forms an image by reflection is a mirror. A mirror does not transmit light but reflects it. When light strikes a mirror, it forms an angle called the angle of incidence. The reflected beam also forms an angle called the angle of reflection. These angles are always equal. Thus light beams that strike a mirror in a certain pattern are reflected as an image of that pattern.

Spherical mirrors produce images that are magnified or reduced. Mirrors for applying facial makeup, for example, produce

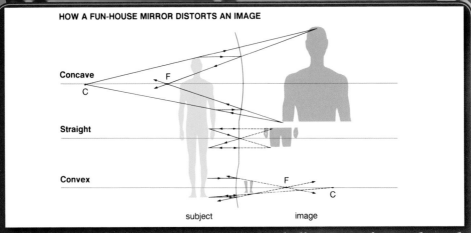

HOW A FUN-HOUSE MIRROR DISTORTS AN IMAGE

Concave

F

C

Straight

Convex

F

C

subject

image

A fun-house mirror at an amusement park distorts an image through a combination of convex and concave surfaces. The image can be either greatly magnified or diminished in appearance. **Encyclopædia Britannica, Inc.**

a magnified image, but some rear-vision mirrors for automobiles are spherical in the opposite manner and produce images that are reduced. Cylindrical mirrors focus a parallel beam of light to a line focus, making the image appear thinner than the real object. A parabolic mirror may be used to focus parallel rays to a real focus, as in a telescope mirror, or to produce a parallel beam from a source at its focus, as in a searchlight. An ellipsoidal mirror will reflect light from one of its two focal points to the other, and an object situated at the focus of a hyperbolic mirror will have a virtual image.

In ancient times mirrors were polished pieces of brass, gold, and silver. Since the 1600s most mirrors have been made from plate glass. The front surface of the glass is highly polished. The rear surface has a metallic reflecting film applied to it. Glass mirrors may be plane or curved. A plane mirror has a flat surface and forms a true image. A curved mirror may have convex or concave surfaces to concentrate light beams or to form distorted images. The most important commercial use of plate-glass mirrors is as decorative fixtures in homes and offices.

The curved surface of a magnifying lens, which can be seen in the light reflecting off of it. Hemera/Thinkstock

from air to water or from glass to air—it bends at the interface (where the two surfaces meet). This bending is called refraction. The amount, or degree, of refraction is related to the difference between the speeds of light in the two materials of different densities—the greater the difference in densities, the more the speed changes, and the greater the bend. A slanting object partly out of water displays refraction. The object appears to bend at the interface of the air and water. Lenses refract light. Those that have concave, or hollowed-out, surfaces spread light rays apart. Those that have convex, or bulging, surfaces bring light rays closer together.

For centuries before the 1600s, scientists had known that when a ray of white light shines on a prism, a broad band containing several colors emerges. Some thought that the colors were caused by variations in lightness and darkness. But in 1672 Isaac Newton published the results of his experiments with light. He showed that a second prism placed in the path of a beam of one color could not add more color to the beam. It did, however, spread the beam farther apart. Newton concluded that the first prism broke white light down into its separate parts by spreading

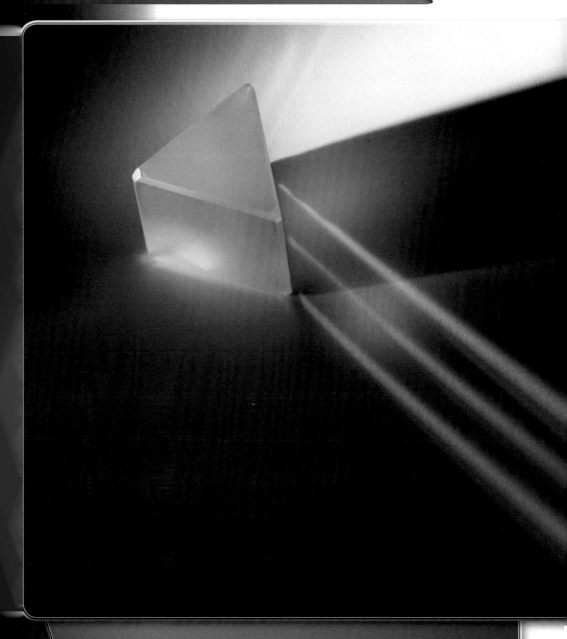

A prism separates white light into its component colors. Milan B/
Shutterstock.com

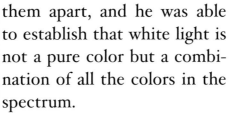

them apart, and he was able to establish that white light is not a pure color but a combination of all the colors in the spectrum.

A prism spreads white light into the spectrum because each color has a slightly different speed within the prism, so each color bends (refracts) a slightly different amount as it enters and again as it leaves the prism. Violet light slows up the most, so it is bent the most; red light slows up the least, so it is bent the least. This spreading apart of white light into a spectrum is called dispersion.

Physicists often define dispersion as the fact that different colors move at different speeds within a substance, not necessarily causing a spectrum. For example, when white light enters a glass block that has parallel faces, the colors all have different speeds and bend different amounts as they travel through the glass. This is also dispersion. But the colors all bend back to form white light as they leave the second parallel face, so separate colors are not observed.

Opaque materials absorb all the colors of white light except their own, which they reflect. A piece of pure red material absorbs orange, yellow, green, blue, and violet but reflects red. Transparent colored materials absorb all colors except their own, which they both transmit and reflect. A piece of pure blue cellophane absorbs red, orange, yellow, green, and violet but transmits blue (it looks blue on the side opposite the light source) and reflects blue (it looks blue on the same side as the light source).

CHAPTER 3

The Speed of Light

Light can travel through a vacuum. Stars are easily visible on clear nights, though their light must travel for years through empty space before it reaches Earth. A laboratory experiment demonstrates that light can travel through a vacuum. When air is pumped out of a glass vacuum chamber that contains a ringing bell, the bell remains visible while the sound fades away. The vacuum cannot transmit sound waves, but the light rays continue to pass through it.

It is much easier to describe the interaction of light with matter than to explain what light is. One reason for this is that light cannot be seen until it interacts with matter--a beam of light is invisible unless it strikes an eye or unless there are particles that reflect parts of the beam to an eye. Also, light travels very fast--so fast that for centuries people disputed whether it required any time for light to move from one point to another.

EARLY MEASUREMENTS

Galileo suggested one of the first experiments to measure the speed of light, and Italian scientists carried out his idea. Two men were stationed on two hilltops. Each had a shaded lantern. The first man was to uncover his lantern. As soon as the second man saw the light, he was to uncover his lantern. The scientists tried to measure the time that elapsed between the moment the first lantern was uncovered and the moment a return beam was detected. The speed of light was much too fast to be measured in this way, and the scientists therefore concluded that light might well travel instantaneously.

Olaus Roemer, a Danish astronomer, was dealing with a different problem when he came across the first workable method for measuring the speed of light. He was timing the eclipses of Jupiter's moons and noticed that the time between eclipses varied by several minutes. As Earth approached Jupiter, the time between eclipses grew shorter. As Earth receded from Jupiter, the time between eclipses grew longer. In 1676 Roemer proposed that these discrepancies be used to calculate the time required for light to travel the diameter of Earth's orbit. Since the exact size of Earth's orbit was not yet known, and since Jupiter's irregular surface caused errors in timing the eclipses, he did not arrive at an accurate value for the speed of light. But

Hubble Telescope composite image of Jupiter with the shadows of its moons. NASA, ESA, and E. Karkoschka (University of Arizona)

he had demonstrated that light took time to travel and that its speed was too quick to measure on Earth with the instruments then available.

In 1849 Armand Fizeau, a French physicist, devised a way to measure the speed of light on Earth instead of relying on uncertain astronomical measurements. His experimental apparatus included a beam of light that was sent through a notch in a rotating disk, was reflected from a mirror, and returned to the disk. The disk had 720 notches. When the returning light passed through a notch, an observer could detect it; if it hit between notches, the light was eclipsed. The distance light would travel (from the open notch to the mirror and back to the point where a tooth could eclipse the light) was measured. Fizeau timed the eclipses and observed the rotational speed of the disk at the time of the eclipses. With this information he calculated that the speed of light in air was 194,000 miles per second. Later investigators refined this method. Jean Foucault replaced the disk with rotating mirrors and arrived at a value of 186,000 miles per second.

THE MICHELSON-MORLEY EXPERIMENT

One of the most surprising and confusing facts about light was discovered by Albert Michelson and Edward Morley. They measured the speed of light very accurately as it traveled both in the same direction as Earth's movement and in the direction opposite to Earth's movement. They expected to get

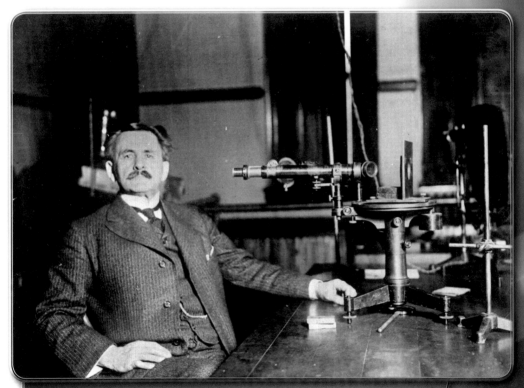

Albert Michelson in his laboratory. **Boyer/Roger Viollet/ Getty Images**

slightly different values, believing that the speed of Earth would be added to or subtracted from the speed of light. The situation, as they saw it, was similar to that of a person looking out the window of a car traveling at 60 miles (96 kilometers) per hour. If another car going 80 miles (128 kilometers) per hour overtakes it, the second car then seems to be moving at a speed of 20 miles (32 kilometers) per hour, or its own speed *minus* the speed of the car it has passed. If a car going 80 miles per hour approaches a car going 60 miles per hour, it seems to be traveling at 140 miles (224 kilometers) per hour, or its own speed *plus* the speed of the car that it is approaching. Light, the two men discovered, does not behave that way. Its speed appears to be the same, no matter what the speed or direction of movement of the observer making the measurement. Albert Einstein developed his theory of special relativity to help explain this phenomenon.

FUNDAMENTAL CONSTANT OF NATURE

The accepted value for the speed of light in a vacuum is 299,792,458 meters per second (about 186,282 miles per second), a

Albert Einstein. Hulton Archive/Getty Images

fundamental constant of the universe. According to the theory of special relativity, time and distance may change as the speed of an object approaches the speed of light (its length shrinks and any changes it regularly undergoes take longer to occur, relative to a stationary observer), but the measured value for the speed of light is constant.

CHAPTER 4

PARTICLE AND WAVE THEORIES

By the 17th century enough was known about the behavior of light for two conflicting theories of its structure to emerge. One theory held that a light ray was made up of a stream of tiny particles. The other regarded light as a wave. Both of these views have been incorporated into the modern theory of light.

Newton thought that light was composed of tiny particles given off by light sources. He believed that the different colors into which white light could be broken up were formed by particles of different sizes. He thought refraction resulted from the stronger attraction of the denser of two substances for the particles of light. Since the attraction was greater, the speed of light in denser mediums should also be greater, according to his theory.

A basic piece of evidence supporting the particle view of light is that light travels in

The clearly defined edges of a shadow. iStockphoto/Thinkstock

straight lines. This can be seen when a small, steady light source shines on a relatively large object. The shadow of the object has sharp borders. Newton felt that if light were a wave, it would curve slightly around obstacles, giving fuzzy-edged shadows. He pointed out that water waves curve as they pass an obstacle (for example, dock pilings) and that sound waves curve over hills and around the corners

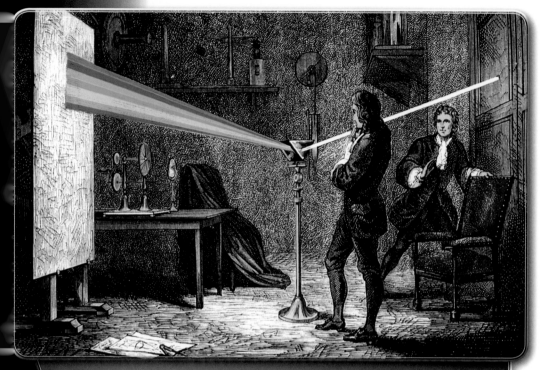

Illustration of Isaac Newton experimenting with a prism.
Apic/Hulton Archive/Getty Images

of buildings. Newton realized, however, that simple variations in the size of particles did not explain all light phenomena. When he tried to understand the shimmering coloration of soap bubbles, he had to introduce the idea that the particles vibrated. Christiaan Huygens, a Dutch physicist, proposed that light was a wave. He postulated that a substance called the ether (not to be confused with the class of chemicals called ethers) filled the universe. Waves were generated in this substance when light traveled through it. Huygens assumed that light waves were like sound waves—the movement of alternately compressed and rarefied ether. Such waves are called longitudinal waves because the vibration of the wave is parallel to the direction in which it is traveling.

POLARIZED LIGHT

Neither particle nor wave theory could really explain the polarization of light by certain transparent crystals. Both Newton and Huygens knew that when light was directed through certain crystals, it would emerge much dimmer. If a second crystal of this class were placed at a certain angle in the path of the dimmed light, the light could pass through it. Then, as either of the two crystals was slowly turned, the light emerging from the second crystal grew dimmer until it was completely blocked. Evidently, something in the structure of the first crystal allowed only part of the light to pass. When the second crystal was lined up properly with the first, it allowed the same amount of light to pass; when it was at the wrong angle to the first

Christiaan Huygens. Leemage/Universal Image Group/ Getty Images

crystal, it screened out the light from the first crystal.

Newton speculated that polarization occurred because light particles had various shapes on their sides, some of which were rejected by the crystal structure. This was not a very satisfactory explanation. However, Huygens had to make even more complicated assumptions to explain how crystals could polarize longitudinal waves. Neither the wave theory nor the particle theory was sufficiently developed to account for all the observed light phenomena, but the weight of Newton's reputation caused the particle theory to be accepted by most scientists.

LIGHT BENDS AROUND CORNERS

In the early 19th century Thomas Young, a British physician, took the next step in developing the wave theory. He demonstrated that light waves were so short that the amount they curved as they passed an object was too small to be visible. He showed that, though shadows from point sources of light appear to have sharp edges, there are thin light-and-dark bands along their borders that are caused by the bending of some light rays into the shadow.

This scattering of light, called diffraction, can be observed under certain conditions. A thin tubular source, such as a fluorescent light, is good. A very thin slit in an opaque material, or even two fingers squeezed loosely together so that light may pass between them, may cause diffraction. The slit is held a foot or two in front of one eye, parallel to the light source; the other eye is closed. Light shines through the slit, and a pattern of colored bands, or a colored glow, can be seen outlining the slit. The outline is colored because diffraction disperses white light into its separate colors in much the same way that a prism does. Young observed diffraction and concluded that it occurred because light was a wave.

Three important measurements describe a wave—speed, frequency, and wavelength. Frequency is a measure of the number of waves that pass a given point in a specified amount of time. Wavelength is the distance from one crest (the highest point) to the next crest, or from one trough (the lowest point) to the next. If all the waves have the same speed, a great many short waves will pass a point in the same time that only a few long waves pass it. Speed equals the wavelength times the frequency.

Interference pattern in a ripple tank. **Andrew Lambert Photography/Photo Researchers, Inc.**

Young set up an experiment to measure the wavelength of light, using the principle of interference. When two sets of waves meet, they interfere with each other in a predictable way. Water waves, such as those made by the wakes of two boats, illustrate this. When two wakes meet, the water becomes choppy. Parts of the waves are very high and parts are very low; the individual waves can reinforce each other or cancel each other. Where two crests meet, the wave becomes higher. Where two troughs meet, the wave becomes deeper. And if a crest and a trough meet, they cancel each other and the water is level.

In his interference experiment, Young used a single light source, a pinhole that admitted a single beam of sunlight. This beam fell on a screen that had two pinholes close together. As light passed through each pinhole, it curved and spread out (diffracted). Because the pinholes were close enough together, the two light beams met and interfered with each other. Their interference pattern was seen on a screen behind the pinholes. With this pattern and knowing the distance between the screens, Young was able to calculate that the wavelength of visible light was about one millionth of a meter.

Subsequent measurements show that the wavelengths of visible light range from 2.99×10^{-5} inches to 1.51×10^{-5} inches (7.60×10^{-5} centimeters to 3.85×10^{-5} centimeters). Each color is associated with a

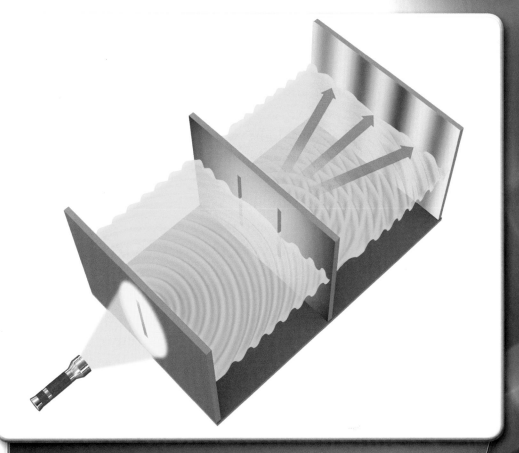

An illustration shows the concept of interference of light. Light passes first through a single slit and then through closely set double slits. Upon passing through the double slits, the light beams spread apart and overlap. In the area of overlap, bands of bright light alternate with bands of darkness. **Dorling Kindersley RF/Thinkstock**

range of wavelengths. Red has the longest lengths. The wavelengths decrease from orange through yellow, green, blue, and violet.

TRANSVERSE WAVES
EXPLAIN POLARIZATION

Young and Augustin-Jean Fresnel, a French physicist, cooperated in developing the idea that light waves are transverse, that they resemble the waves made when a rope stretched from a post is jerked up and down, rather than longitudinal sound waves. The rope itself moves only up and down, at right angles to the forward travel of the wave. Young and Fresnel suggested the wave motion of light might also be at right angles to the direction in which the wave was traveling. The motion could be in any direction between sideways and up and down just so long as it was at right angles to the direction of travel. Wave motion of this kind could explain polarization. If a polarizing crystal admitted only those waves that were vibrating in a certain direction, then a second crystal would block those waves if it were turned at an angle to the first. The second one would be oriented to accept only waves vibrating in a different direction, and the first crystal would have already blocked all those waves. Fresnel made calculations that accounted for all the light behavior he knew

The filters in polarized sunglassess block certain light waves that can cause glare. Yusia/Shutterstock.com

of by assuming that light was made up of transverse waves.

Measurements of the speed of light in substances other than air presented additional difficulties for Newton's particle theory of light. The theory had assumed that light travels faster in dense substances than in rarefied substances. Fizeau and Foucault measured the speed of light in various transparent substances and discovered that it was slower in denser materials than in air.

Invisible Light

Around 1800—while Young was developing his wave theory—three scientists discovered that the color spectrum was bordered by invisible rays. Sir William Herschel, a British astronomer, was measuring the temperature of the colors dispersed by a prism. As he moved the thermometer down the spectrum from violet to red, he observed a rise in temperature. As he moved the thermometer beyond the red beam, the temperature grew even higher. Herschel had discovered a hot, invisible radiation that appeared to be a continuation of the spectrum. This radiation is called infrared radiation because it

Thermal camera image of a face. Thermal imaging makes use of the infrared radiation emitted by objects. **Edward Kinsman/ Photo Researchers/Getty Images**

occurs just below red in the spectrum, where there is no visible light.

Ultraviolet rays were discovered by Johann Wilhelm Ritter and by William Hyde Wollaston, who were independently studying the effects of light on silver chloride. Silver chloride placed in violet light grew dark. When the chemical was placed in the area beyond the violet of the spectrum, it

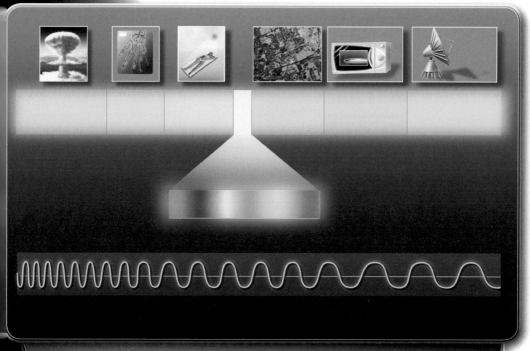

Illustration of the progression of wavelength on the electromagnetic spectrum, ranging from gamma rays (left), with the shortest wavelength, to radio waves, with the longest wavelength. **BSIP/ Photo Researchers, Inc.**

darkened even more rapidly. They concluded that a chemically powerful kind of invisible radiation lay beyond the violet end of the spectrum.

In 1864 James Clerk Maxwell, a Scottish physicist, published a theory of electricity and magnetism. He had developed equations that predicted the existence of electromagnetic waves caused by electrical disturbances. He calculated the speed of such waves and found it to be the same as the speed of light. Maxwell concluded that light was an electromagnetic wave. As a single light wave travels through space, its movement consists of the growth and collapse of electrical and magnetic fields. The electrical fields are at right angles to the magnetic fields, and both are at right angles to the direction in which the wave is moving.

Maxwell's theory implied that other electromagnetic radiations with wavelengths longer than infrared or shorter than ultraviolet might be found. In 1887 Heinrich Hertz produced radio waves, which have longer wavelengths than infrared rays, thus confirming Maxwell's theory.

CHAPTER 5

LIGHT: WAVE AND PARTICLE

By the end of the 19th century the battle over the nature of light as a wave or a collection of particles seemed over. James Clerk Maxwell's theory of electromagnetism and Heinrich Hertz's discovery of electromagnetic waves were great triumphs in support of wave theory. However, just when everything seemed to be settled, a period of revolutionary change was ushered in at the beginning of the 20th century. The advent of quantum theory once again reopened the question of the nature of light. Eventually it was determined that both the wave theory and the particle theory were needed to explain the properties of light.

QUANTUM THEORY OF LIGHT

In 1900 the German physicist Max Planck advanced a theory to account for the

Max Planck. **Science Source/Photo Researchers/Getty Images**

behavior of blackbodies. A blackbody is an ideal substance with a perfectly black surface that absorbs all the radiation that falls on it and emits radiation in specific ways dependent on temperature. While such an ideal material does not actually exist, some materials resemble it closely enough to provide experimental tests of blackbody theory. The observed behavior is that blackbodies do not emit all wavelengths in equal amounts. Instead, certain wavelengths are emitted more often than others. As the temperature increases, the wavelengths that are emitted preferentially decrease in length. In other words, the wavelength of maximum emission varies inversely with temperature. Planck explained this behavior by suggesting that matter can handle energy only in specific amounts, called quanta, and that amounts of energy between these quanta cannot be absorbed or emitted.

In 1905 Einstein expanded this idea in his explanation of the photoelectric effect. If light falls on certain metals, electrons in those metals are freed and can form an electric current. Einstein was trying to account for the observation that the energy of the electrons is independent of the amount of

THE ORIGINS OF SPECTRUM ANALYSIS

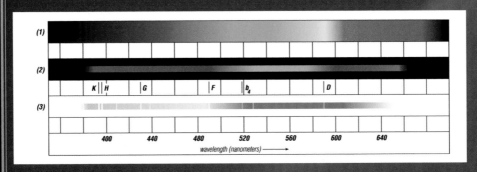

A continuous-emission spectrum from an ordinary incandescent lamp is shown in number 1. Number 2 depicts a "mixed" spectrum of the sun with an absorption (dark-line) spectrum characteristic of the cooler outer layers of the sun superimposed upon the continuous-emission spectrum of the sun's hotter, inner layers. The letters mark Fraunhofer lines, which are characteristic spectroscopic lines caused by the sun's gases: sodium (D), iron and magnesium (b_4), hydrogen (F), iron and calcium (G), and calcium (H,K). Number 3 shows a negative of film 2. The film is darker where it has been more exposed; therefore, the previously black absorption line now appears white. Encyclopædia Britannica, Inc.

The spectral pattern of light is different for various classes of light sources. Light from the Sun, from certain lamp filaments, and from molten metals each produces a spectrum that has all colors in an unbroken array. Such a pattern is called a continuous spectrum. Incandescent gases give off only certain colors, in fine lines. Their spectra are called bright-line spectra.

In the early 1800s Joseph von Fraunhofer observed that the continuous spectrum was crossed by many dark lines. He charted more than 700 of them, but he was unable to explain their meaning. Because of his discovery, however, they are called Fraunhofer lines.

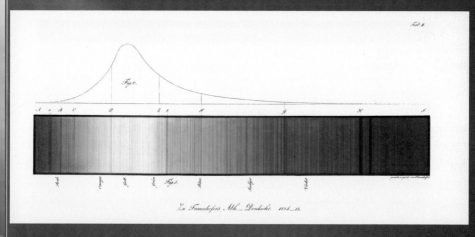

Joseph von Fraunhofer's diagram of the solar spectrum, showing the dark lines now known as Fraunhofer lines. © Science Faction/SuperStock

The meaning of the Fraunhofer lines was discovered about 50 years later by Gustav Kirchhoff and Robert Bunsen. With an instrument called a spectroscope, they studied the spectra of certain substances that were vaporized in the nonluminous Bunsen burner flame. Each vapor showed a characteristic bright-line spectrum. But when emitted light was passed through a cooler vapor of the same substance, the bright lines were replaced by dark ones in the same position.

This replacement of bright by dark lines meant that the second vapor had absorbed the characteristic light of the first. Later experiments showed that the cooler vapor absorbs those light waves that it would normally emit at a higher temperature.

Kirchhoff and Bunsen also noticed that characteristic arrays of lines are given off by the different chemical elements. For example, incandescent sodium always gives certain yellow lines near the middle of the spectrum, and no other element gives these lines. Thus when these lines appear, sodium must be present in the incandescent substance. If the lines are bright, the light has come directly from the incandescent sodium. If they are dark, the light has passed, somewhere along its path, through an absorbing vapor containing some gaseous sodium. Only minute quantities of an element are needed to make its lines appear. This makes it possible to identify the elements in unknown substances.

radiation falling on the metal. The maximum energy of the electrons was observed to depend on the wavelength of the radiation. Einstein suggested that the photoelectric effect could also be accounted for by assuming that electromagnetic energy, including light, always occurs in these bundles. This reintroduced the particle theory. The results of many subsequent experiments supported the idea that light energy travels in quanta. An individual light particle possesses one quantum of energy and is called a photon.

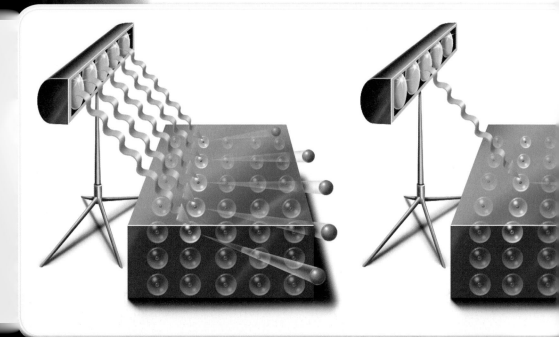

Illustration of the photoelectric effect. **BSIP/Photo Researchers, Inc.**

ELEMENTS AND THEIR SPECTRA

The way matter becomes a light source can be explained in terms of quantum theory. When certain elements are heated, they give off light of a specific color. This light can be separated into a spectrum that is made up of many distinct bright lines. Each element has its unique spectrum, which can be accurately measured. Since a spectrum

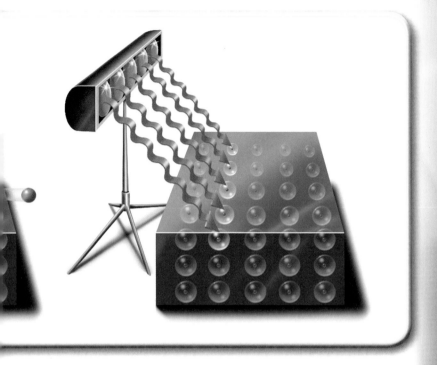

positively identifies each element, the chemical composition of astronomical bodies is determined by an analysis of their spectra.

Scientists wondered why the atoms of each element, when provided with a wide range of energies by the heating process, give off only the specific energies in their spectra. The modern theory of atomic structure makes this phenomenon understandable. An atom is made up of a heavy, positively charged nucleus that is surrounded by light, negatively charged electrons.

Modern theory states that the electrons of an atom can assume certain fixed energy relationships, called energy levels, to one another and to the nucleus. These energy levels are the same for all the atoms of an element. An electron must occupy one of the energy levels; it cannot possess any energy between levels.

When an atom is heated, enough energy may be given to one of the electrons to raise it to a higher energy level. But it usually jumps back to a lower level, giving off an electromagnetic wave, which is the energy difference of the two levels. When this energy is in the visible light range, it shows up as one of the lines in the element's visible spectrum. Each element has a different spectrum because each element has a different number of electrons and different energy levels available to these electrons.

THE DUAL NATURE OF LIGHT

In the early 20th century atomic theory had not yet explained why both a wave theory and a particle theory were needed to describe light. Physicists used both, depending on which was more useful in a given situation. The paradox was finally resolved in 1924 by Louis de Broglie. He postulated that matter, which had always been treated as a collection of particles, had a wave aspect as well. This wave nature has been demonstrated in experiments with such particles as electrons.

Conclusion

Light is fundamental to life on Earth. Sunlight, through its role in photosynthesis, is essential to the food chain, and in early human history it provided the only light to make sight possible. Later, the harnessing of light—from the fires of cave dwellers to the invention of the electric lamp—revolutionized the way people lived and worked. Thus it is no surprise that people have always sought to understand the true nature of this crucial form of energy.

As this volume has shown, the subject of light has occupied some of the world's most prominent scientists. For centuries the basic question about light—whether it was a wave or a stream of particles—went unresolved, with such notables as Isaac Newton and Christiaan Huygens on opposite sides of the debate. Even after wave theory gained consensus in the 1800s, ongoing mysteries about the emission of light led Max Planck, in what he called an "act of desperation," to propose the revolutionary quantum theory of light in 1900. His work, soon built upon by

Albert Einstein and others, led to the eventual acceptance of the wave-particle duality of light. It also formed the basis of quantum mechanics, the branch of physics that deals with the behavior of matter and light at the atomic and subatomic levels. One of the great ideas of the 20th century, quantum mechanics continues to be at the forefront of advances in physics today.

Glossary

bioluminescence The emission of light from living organisms.

candela The base unit of luminous intensity in the International System of Units.

concave Hollowed or rounded inward like the inside of a bowl.

convex Curved or rounded outward like the exterior of a sphere or circle.

diffraction A modification that light undergoes, especially in passing by the edges of opaque bodies or through narrow openings and in which the rays appear to be deflected.

dispersion The separation of light into colors by refraction or diffraction with formation of a spectrum.

electron An elementary particle consisting of a charge of negative electricity.

energy A fundamental entity of nature that is transferred between parts of a system in the production of physical change within the system and usually regarded as the capacity for doing work.

ether The rarefied element formerly believed to fill the upper regions of space.

fluorescence Luminescence that is caused by the absorption of radiation at one wavelength followed by nearly immediate re-radiation usually at a different wavelength and that stops almost at once when the incident radiation stops.

foot-candle A unit of illumination on a surface that is equal to one lumen per square foot.

frequency A measure of the number of waves that pass a given point in a specified amount of time.

gamma ray Electromagnetic radiation of the shortest wavelength and highest energy.

incandescence The emission by a hot body of radiation that makes it visible.

lumen A unit of luminous flux, or amount of light.

luminous Emitting or reflecting light.

microwave Electromagnetic radiation with a wavelength between one millimeter and one meter.

opaque Blocking the passage of radiant energy and especially light.

photoelectric effect The emission of free electrons from a metal surface when light strikes it.

photon An individual light particle possessing one quantum of energy.

photosynthesis The process by which green plants and some other organisms use sunlight to produce food and oxygen.

polarization The action or process of affecting radiation and especially light so that the vibrations of the wave assume a definite form.

prism A piece of glass or other transparent material cut with precise angles and plane faces, useful for analyzing and reflecting light.

quantum Any of the very small increments or parcels into which many forms of energy are subdivided.

radio frequency wave Form of electromagnetic radiation with the longest wavelengths.

refraction The change in direction of a wave in passing from one medium (as air) into another (as glass) in which its speed is different.

relativity Wide-ranging physical theories formed by Albert Einstein that explain how physical laws and measurements change when considered by observers in various states of motion.

steradian A unit of measure of solid angles.

translucent Transmitting and diffusing light so that objects beyond cannot be seen clearly.

transparent Transmitting light without appreciable scattering so that objects beyond are seen clearly.

ultraviolet radiation Electromagnetic radiation having wavelengths shorter than those of visible light and longer than those of X-rays.

watt Unit of power equal to the work done at the rate of one joule per second or to the power produced by a current of one ampere across a potential difference of one volt.

wavelength The distance between the peaks or valleys of two consecutive waves.

American Physical Society
One Physics Ellipse
College Park, MD 20740-3844
(301) 209-3200
Web site: http://www.aps.org
The American Physical Society is an organization that allows physicists to collaborate and share the latest information in their field.

Institute of Physics
76 Portland Place
London W1B 1NT
United Kingdom
+44 (0)20 7470 4800
Web site: http://www.iop.org
The Institute of Physics is a London-based organization that works to advance physics research and education.

NASA
Public Communications Office
Suite 5K39
Washington, DC 20546-0001
(202) 358-0001
Web site: http://www.nasa.gov
NASA is the U.S. agency committed to space exploration and study.

The Science Club
4921 Preston/Fall-City Road
Fall City, WA 98024
(425) 222-5066
Web site: http://www.scienceclub.org
The Science Club offers science experiments to elementary school students, teachers, and parents through school assemblies, parent and teacher workshops, television, video, and print.

WEB SITES

Due to the changing nature of Internet links, Rosen Educational Services has developed an online list of Web sites related to the subject of this book. This site is updated regularly. Please use this link to access the list:

www.rosenlinks.com/inphy/light

Anderson, L.W. *Light and Color*, rev. ed. (Raintree, 1991).

Asimov, Isaac. *How Did We Find Out About the Speed of Light?* (Walker, 1986).

Bortz, A. B. *The Photon* (Rosen, 2004).

Bova, Ben. *The Story of Light* (Sourcebooks, 2002).

Burnie, David. *Light* (Dorling Kindersley, 2000).

Cobb, Vicki, and Cobb, Josh. *Light Action!: Amazing Experiments with Optics* (SPIE, 2005).

Gardner, Robert. *Easy Genius Science Projects with Light: Great Experiments and Ideas* (Enslow, 2009).

Hecht, Jeff. *Optics: Light for a New Age* (Optical Society of America, 2000).

Waldman, Gary. *Introduction to Light* (Dover, 2002).

Wood, R.W. *Light Fundamentals* (Chelsea House, 1999).

W

wave theory of light, 40,
    42–43, 45–49, 50–52,
    56, 64–65, 66
Wollaston, William
    Hyde, 54

X

X-rays, 11, 16

Y

Young, Thomas, 45, 46,
    47–48, 50, 52